MEN EXPOSED

⊗

A Heartless Little Book

Pat Ross

A FIRESIDE BOOK
Published by Simon & Schuster

FIRESIDE
Rockefeller Center
1230 Avenue of the Americas
New York, NY 10020

Manufactured in the United States of America

1 3 5 7 9 10 8 6 4 2

Library of Congress Cataloging-in-Publication Data
Ross, Pat, date.
Men exposed : a heartless little book / Pat Ross.
        p.   cm.
        "A Fireside book."
I. Men—Humor. 2. Man-woman relationships—Humor. I. Title.

PN6231.M45R665   1999

818'.5402—dc21   99-10530
                                         CIP

ISBN 0-684-85218-7

Photo credits:

The Museum of Modern Art Film Stills Archive for page 57.

Courtesy of the Academy of Motion Picture Arts and Sciences
for pages 6, 13, 17, 25, 29, 33, 35, 47, 49, 53, 55, 65, 67, 89.

The Kobal Collection for pages 9, 51.

The British Film Institute for pages 2, 11, 31.

For page 39: copyright © 1999 by Universal City Studios, Inc.
Courtesy of Universal Studios Publishing Rights. All Rights Reserved.

Women agree that the perfect man would . . .

Share the housework.

Stop sulking when he doesn't get his way.

👉

Be the one to do the grocery list.

Not get so worked up when you're running late.

Stop treating you like he owns you.

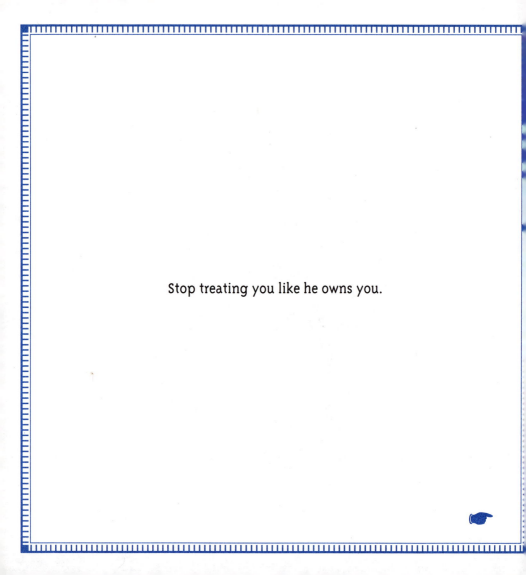

Never have to be reminded of your birthday and anniversary.

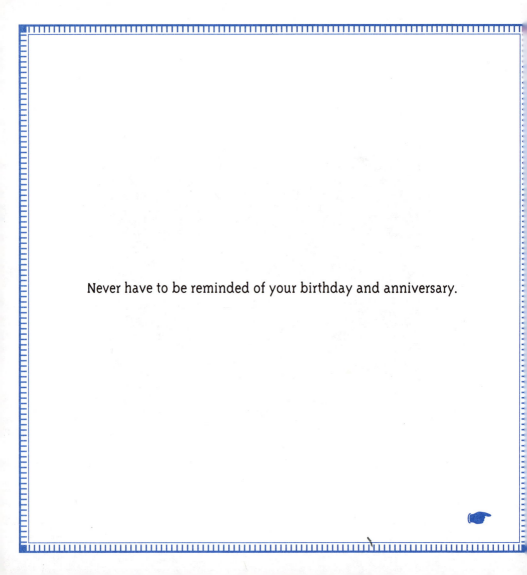

Plan an unusual vacation.

Admit he's wrong.

Stop teasing your cat.

Never make you wonder if he'll call or write.

Take better care of his nails.

Act a little more interested around your best friend.

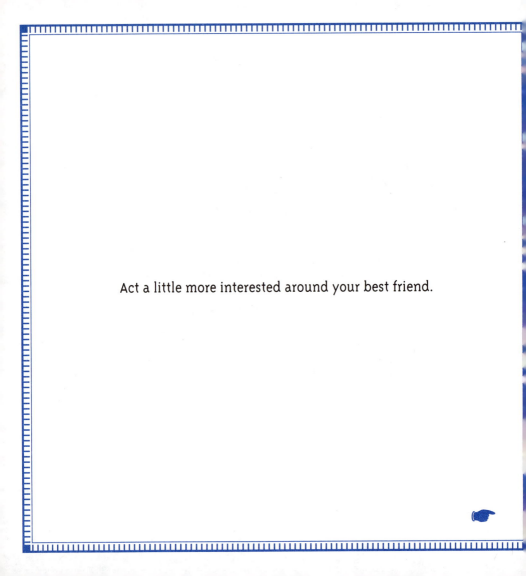

Get it himself!

Tell you what really goes on during Boys' Night Out.

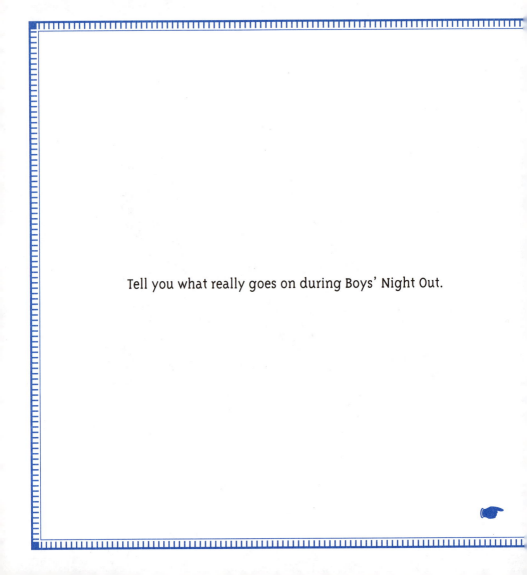

Stop idolizing his mother.

A 104-51

Take a little more interest in decorating.

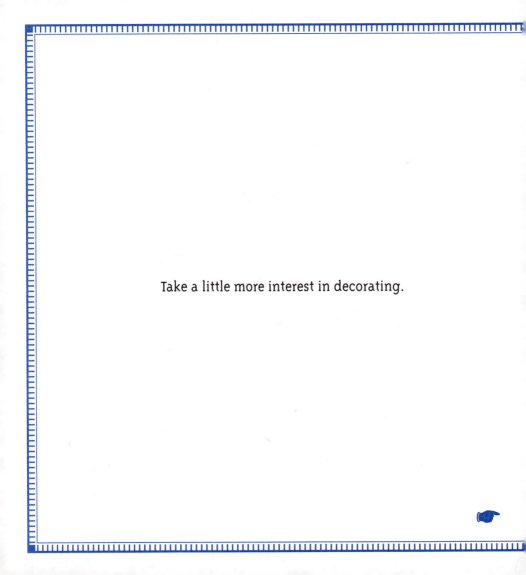

Give you nice things without expecting a payback.

Enjoy games that both of you can win.

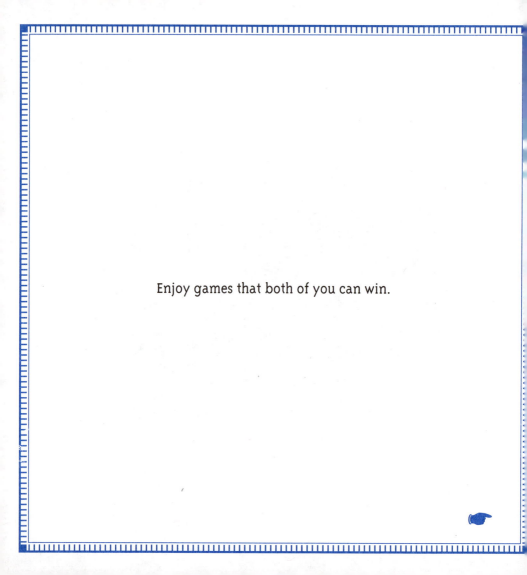

Get a suit that fits.

Not get so hung up on length.

Wine you and dine you more often.

Admit that women make good doctors.

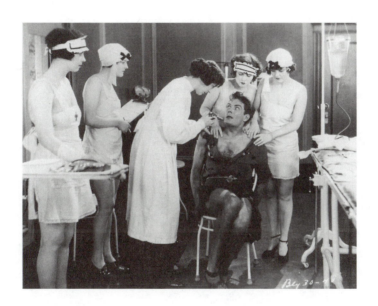

Stop to ask for directions.

Stay out of your closet.

Figure out that he's the problem.

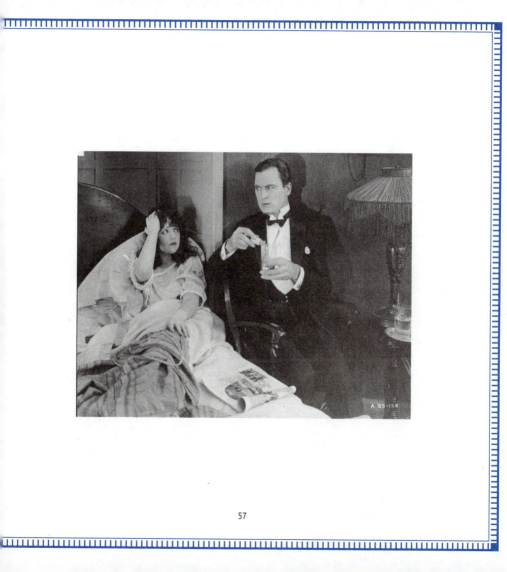

Stop saying he just needs more time.

Never complain that you spend too much time on the phone.

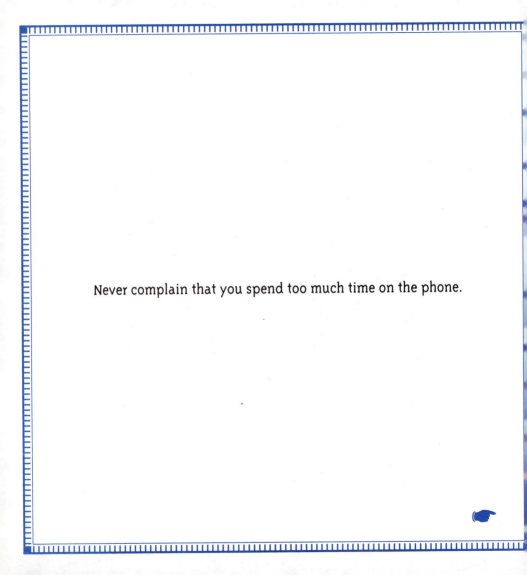

Act his age.

Be content with a light dinner.

Be more supportive.

Come up with creative foreplay.

Stop using the office as an excuse.

Share the paper.

Never suggest that you ask for his mother's recipes.

Learn to lose gracefully.

Get in touch with his feminine side.

Keep his eyes on the road.

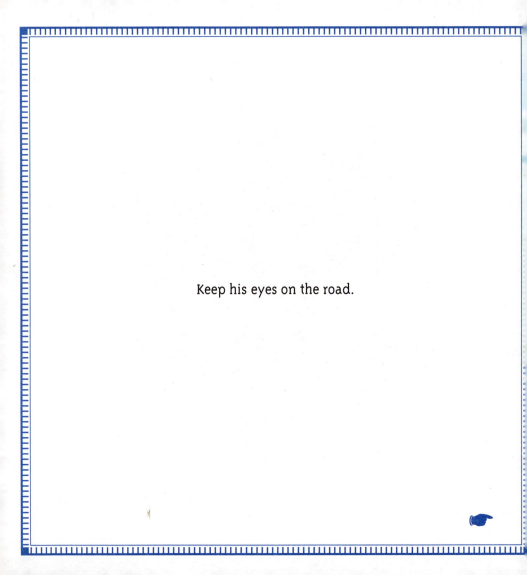

Be willing to hold your handbag in public.

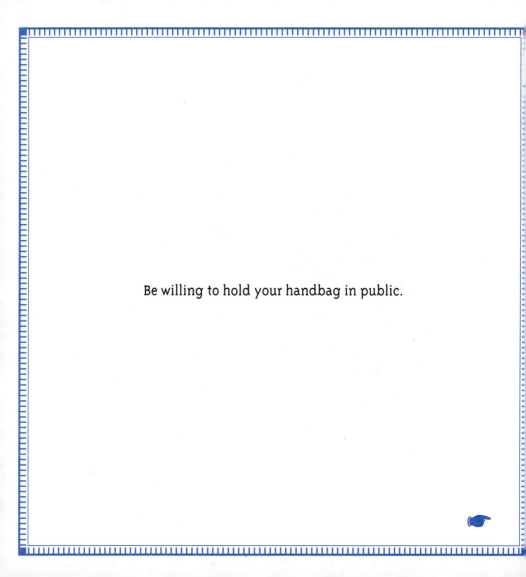

Remember to tell you how nice you look.

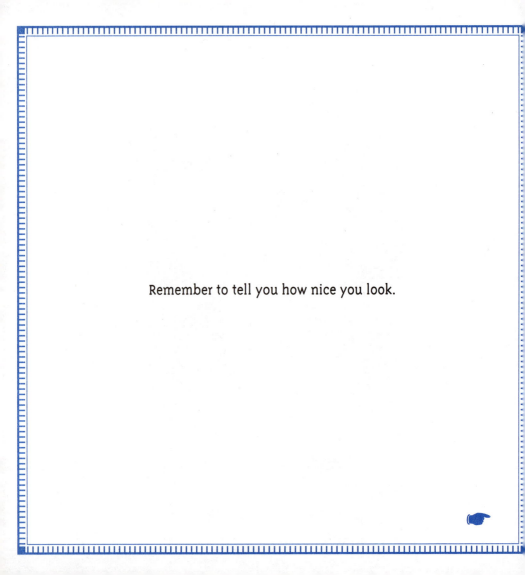

Say, "Sure, give me the comb. I'll fix the back."

Cultivate a taste for flavored teas.

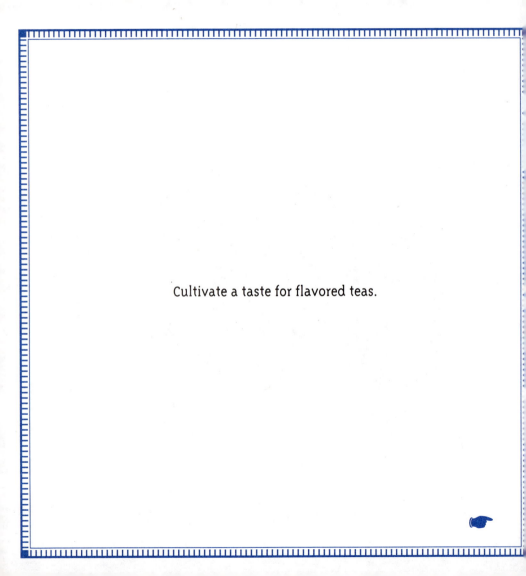

Seek new friends.

Never break your heart.

Always adore you.